ENDANGERED ANIMALS

CHIMPANZEES

BY KRISTEN POPE

Published by The Child's World®
1980 Lookout Drive • Mankato, MN 56003-1705
800-599-READ • www.childsworld.com

Acknowledgments
The Child's World®: Mary Berendes, Publishing Director
Red Line Editorial: Editorial direction and production
The Design Lab: Design
Amnet: Production

Design Element: Shutterstock Images
Photographs ©: Marc L. Schauer/Shutterstock Images, cover, 1; Ronnie Howard/Shutterstock Images, 4, 22; Sam DCruz/Shutterstock Images, 6–7; Norma Cornes/Hemera/Thinkstock, 9; Kjersti Joergensen/Shutterstock Images, 10; Tom Brakefield/Stockbyte/Thinkstock, 11; Bethany Fank/iStockphoto, 12–13; Shutterstock Images, 15, 20; Robin Nieuwenkamp/Shutterstock Images, 16; iStockphoto, 18–19; Rick Roycroft/AP Images, 21

Copyright © 2016 by The Child's World®
All rights reserved. No part of this book may be reproduced or utilized in any form or by any means without written permission from the publisher.

ISBN 9781631439674
LCCN 2014959771

Printed in the United States of America
Mankato, MN
July, 2015
PA02264

ABOUT THE AUTHOR

Kristen Pope is a writer and editor with years of experience working in national and state parks and museums. She has taught people of all ages about science and the environment, including coaxing reluctant insect lovers to pet Madagascar hissing cockroaches.

TABLE OF CONTENTS

CHAPTER ONE
OUR CLOSEST RELATIVES 4

CHAPTER TWO
CHIMPS IN TROUBLE 11

CHAPTER THREE
SAVING CHIMPS 16

What You Can Do, 22

Glossary, 23

To Learn More, 24

Index, 24

CHAPTER ONE

OUR CLOSEST RELATIVES

A young chimp takes a rest in the trees.

A female chimpanzee wakes up high in the trees in her nest of leaves. She uses her long arms to swing between branches. Soon she moves down to the forest floor. She finds a stick. The chimp uses the stick to dig inside an old log.

Chimpanzees live in central and west Africa.

She drags out a plump grub. Then she pops it into her mouth as a quick snack.

Wild chimpanzees live in Africa. Their territory once covered land in 25 different countries. But now chimps are **extinct** in four of them.

Chimpanzees are humans' closest living animal relatives. They share 98 percent of our **genes**. They are **primates** that can live up to 45 years in the wild.

Adult chimpanzees reach up to 5.5 feet (1.7 m) in height. They can weigh 70 to 130 pounds (32 to 59 kg). These **mammals** use their humanlike hands and long toes to pick things up. They walk using their arms and legs. Chimps often walk on their knuckles.

Chimps spend much of their time eating in the trees.

Chimps spend six to eight hours a day finding food. They find most of their food in trees. Chimpanzees eat all kinds of foods. They mostly eat fruit and plants. But chimps also eat insects, eggs, and meat. Chimps may even eat **carrion**.

Chimpanzees find creative ways to get their food. They shape sticks to use as tools. They push the sticks into ant and termite hills and pull out insects. Chimps slurp insects off the sticks using their tongues and lips. Sometimes chimps smash nutshells with rocks. Then they eat the nuts inside. Or they put handfuls of berries or seeds into their mouths.

Chimps also spend a lot of time in family groups. Together they look for food and fight off intruders. Up to

INTELLIGENT ANIMALS

Chimpanzees communicate in many different ways. They kiss, tickle, touch hands, and more. They also talk to each other, and to people, using their hands. Scientists have figured out 66 chimp signals. Some meanings include "follow me" and "stop that."

150 chimps may live in one family group. These big groups are often made of many small families. Each family may have six to ten chimps, including young ones. When they are born, chimpanzees weigh only 4 pounds (2 kg). Infant chimps ride on their mothers. At first, they clutch her chest. As they get bigger, they ride piggyback style. Infant chimps rely on their mothers until they are about six years old. By the time they are

Chimpanzees are smart animals and use tools to find food.

Mothers and their offspring may stay together for much of their lives.

nine, chimpanzees can take care of themselves. They can find their own food. But they often stay close to their mothers for life.

Chimps are social, intelligent animals. But they are threatened in the wild. People are putting their future at risk.

CHAPTER TWO

CHIMPS IN TROUBLE

The future of chimpanzees is uncertain.

In 1900 there were more than one million wild chimpanzees on Earth. Today there are fewer than 300,000 wild chimpanzees. Now chimpanzees are **endangered**. There are many reasons why.

Chimps have two known **predators**: humans and leopards. Leopards are a natural predator. They kill only as many chimps as they can eat. Humans, however, are a big threat.

People destroy the chimps' forest **habitat**. Humans cut down trees to create fields for growing crops. They use the timber to build homes, furniture, and other items. Other people cut down even more trees to make new roads. Oil drilling also destroys the chimps' habitat. When habitat is destroyed, chimpanzees are forced to move to other areas. These areas are small. Often chimp families are cut off from one another.

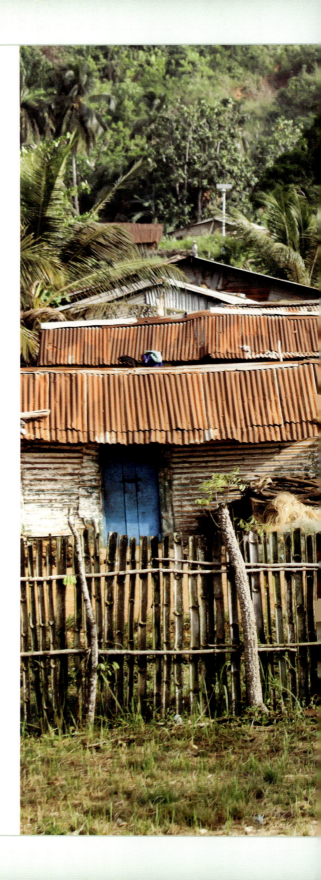

Humans clear chimp habitat to build towns and roads.

Most people do not mean to hurt chimpanzees. Some people do not have much money. They worry about feeding their families. The environment does not seem as important. Some communities do not think there are other ways to make money. Environmental groups and governments try to help them. They teach people new ways to make money. These ways do not hurt the environment or chimps.

It is illegal to kill chimps. But some people break the law. **Poachers** kill chimps for their meat. Chimpanzee meat is considered a special treat by wealthy city dwellers. Poachers also capture infant chimps to sell as pets. Chimpanzee infants are cute and intelligent. But they grow quickly. Adults are stronger than human adults. They can

BUSHMEAT

*In central and western Africa, people hunt forest animals to eat. They have done so for a very long time. This meat is called **bushmeat**. Some people hunt and kill only enough to feed their families. This does not cause a problem for chimp numbers. But others sell the meat. They kill more and more animals to make more money. The number of chimps and other animals decreases. They may become endangered.*

Chimpanzees make poor pets.

bite and destroy property. Despite this, poachers take animals faster than new chimps are born. This causes chimp numbers to decrease.

International law makes killing, selling, and buying chimpanzees illegal. But some police officers do not enforce these laws. Other times, there are not enough police officers. They are busy with other problems.

CHAPTER THREE

SAVING CHIMPS

People and countries are working together to save chimp habitat.

Different countries work together to protect chimpanzees. Working together is important. The chimpanzees' habitat crosses many borders.

In 1973 governments from 80 different countries joined together. They made an agreement. The agreement protects endangered **species**. Countries continue to make their laws stronger. They also enforce existing laws. These laws include rules against poaching and illegal tree cutting.

National parks help protect chimpanzees. Governments set aside national parkland. People are not allowed to cut down the trees. The land is saved as a natural habitat for the animals that live there. Gombe Stream National Park in Tanzania was the first one in Africa. It was created in 1968 to protect chimpanzee habitat. Other groups help with the

Between 2005 and 2013, most of the wild primates killed by humans were chimpanzees.

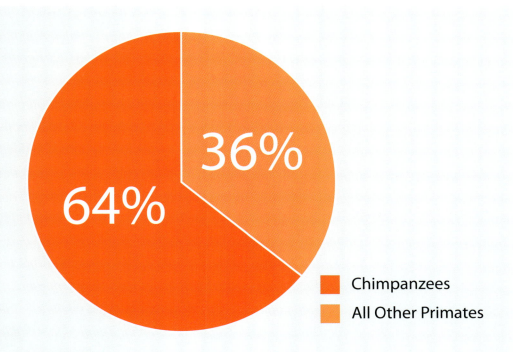

national parks. They raise money to help run the parks. Some groups work to protect habitats that cross countries' borders.

Communities help save chimps, too. Community groups show people how to make money in ways that do not kill chimps. One way is to encourage other people to visit their town. The visitors come to see chimpanzees and other wild animals. This is called **ecotourism**. Community members make money from caring for the animals and their environment.

Chimpanzee families are protected in Gombe Stream National Park.

Scientists are also hard at work. They want to learn more about chimpanzees. One study counts how many chimpanzees live in the wild today. It is hard to know exactly how many live in the forests of Africa. Scientists spend time counting chimps in the wild. Other scientists study chimpanzee behavior. They learn about both chimps and humans.

Ecotourism helps communities make money without harming chimpanzees.

Chimps and humans are closely related species. To save chimpanzees, people must take action. This will prevent our closest relatives from becoming extinct.

Jane Goodall has spent her life studying chimpanzees.

JANE GOODALL

Jane Goodall went to study chimpanzees in Africa more than 50 years ago. She was 26 years old. Today she is one of the world's most famous scientists who studies chimpanzees. She works to protect them through the Jane Goodall Institute.

WHAT YOU CAN DO

- Learn everything you can about chimpanzees and share this information with friends and family.

- Sign a letter to ask the U.S. government to help protect chimpanzees. Jane Goodall has a letter you can e-mail at http://www.janegoodall.org/action.

- Never keep a chimpanzee or another kind of ape or monkey as a pet.

- Have a bake sale and donate the money to the Center for Great Apes.

GLOSSARY

bushmeat (BUSH-meet) Bushmeat is the meat of wild animals that are hunted in the forest. People in Africa have hunted bushmeat for many years.

carrion (KAR-ee-un) Carrion is the flesh of a dead and decaying animal. Chimpanzees will sometimes eat carrion.

ecotourism (eek-oh-TOOR-iz-um) Ecotourism is traveling to natural places in a way that does not hurt animals or the environment. Ecotourism allows people to view chimpanzees in the wild.

endangered (en-DANE-jerd) An endangered animal is in danger of becoming extinct. Chimpanzees are endangered.

extinct (ek-STINKT) If a type of animal is extinct, all the animals have died out. If efforts are not made to save them, chimps may become extinct.

genes (jeenz) Genes are parts of the cells of living things, which determine how a living thing looks, grows, and acts. Chimpanzees share 98 percent of their genes with humans.

habitat (HAB-i-tat) A habitat is a place where an animal lives. A forest is the habitat of chimpanzees.

mammals (MAM-alz) Mammals are animals that are warm-blooded, give birth to live young, and are usually covered with hair. Chimpanzees are mammals.

poachers (PO-churz) Poachers are people who illegally hunt and kill animals. Poachers are a threat to chimpanzees' survival.

predators (PRED-a-terz) Predators hunt, kill, and eat other animals. Chimpanzees have only two predators: humans and leopards.

primates (PRY-mayts) Primates are mammals that have large brains, eyes that can see in three dimensions, and hands and feet that grasp. Humans and chimpanzees are primates.

species (SPEE-sheez) A species is a group of animals that are similar and can produce offspring together. Humans and chimpanzees are similar species.

TO LEARN MORE

BOOKS

Goodall, Jane. *Chimpanzee Children of Gombe*. Chicago: Minedition, 2014.

Marsico, Katie. *Chimpanzees*. New York: Scholastic, 2012.

Winter, Jeanette. *The Watcher: Jane Goodall's Life with the Chimps*. New York: Schwartz & Wade, 2011.

WEB SITES

Visit our Web site for links about chimpanzees:
childsworld.com/links

Note to Parents, Teachers, and Librarians: We routinely verify our Web links to make sure they are safe and active sites. So encourage your readers to check them out!

INDEX

behavior, 4, 6, 8–10
bushmeat, 14

chimpanzee family groups, 8–10
chimpanzees as pets, 14

ecotourism, 18

food, 8

Gombe Stream National Park, 17
Goodall, Jane, 21

habitat, 5, 12, 16–18

national parks, 17–18

poachers, 14, 15
predators, 11

Tanzania, 17
tool use, 8